Nature's Children

PET REPTILES

by Daniel Noonan

Grolier Educational

FACTS IN BRIEF

Classification of reptiles

Class:	*Reptilia* (Reptiles)
Order:	*Squamata* (snakes and lizards), *Chelonia* (turtles)
Suborder:	*Serpentes* (snakes), *Sauria* (lizards)

World distribution. Wild snakes and lizards are found in almost every part of the world.

Habitat. From deserts to rain forests. Pet reptiles are kept in cages and tanks that are like their natural habitats.

Distinctive physical characteristics. Cold-blooded; dry scaly skin. Most reptiles shed their skin as they grow or age.

Habits. Carnivorous reptiles are predators. Most reptiles need to be kept warm with either a heating pad or a basking light.

Diet. Reptiles may be carnivorous (meat-eating), herbivorous (plant-eating), or omnivorous (eat anything).

Library of Congress Cataloging-in Publication Data

Noonan, Daniel. 1973-
    Pet Reptiles / Daniel Noonan.
        p.   cm. — (Nature's children)
    Includes index.
    Summary: Describes the physical characteristics, natural habitat,
behavior, diet, world distribution, domestic types, and care
required of these animals sometimes used as pets.
    ISBN 0-7172-9120-0 (hardbound)
    1. Lizards as pets—Juvenile literature.   2. Reptiles as pets-
-Juvenile literature.   [1. Lizards. 2. Reptiles. 3. Pets.]
I. Title. II. Series.
SF459.L5N66 1997
539.3'9—dc21

97-5950
CIP
AC

This library reinforced edition was published in 1997 exclusively by:

 Grolier Educational

Sherman Turnpike, Danbury, Connecticut 06816

Set ISBN 0-7172-7661-9
Reptiles ISBN 0-7172-9120-0

Contents

2

Reptiles—like this bright green Jackson's chameleon—make unusual but fascinating pets.

Reptiles have been on this planet for longer than just about any other living creature. They come in all sizes, shapes, and colors. Some are fierce, and some are quite peaceful. Some, like gila monsters, beaded lizards, and certain snakes, are poisonous. Others, however, are fascinating creatures that actually can make interesting and wonderful pets.

From the first, though, it should be clear that not all reptiles make good pets. Reptiles that have been captured in the wild, for example, probably should not be kept as pets. They simply are not used to life with people, and as a result, they are likely to be quite difficult to handle. They also can carry diseases or parasites that can harm other pets.

Likewise, poisonous reptiles are not for the inexperienced owner. They are just too dangerous to be kept by someone who is not an expert at dealing with such creatures.

There are many reptiles, however, that do well in captivity, even in people's homes. From colorful geckos to huge snakes, they may be unusual, but they manage to bring many people countless hours of enjoyment.

What Is a Reptile?

For many people reptiles are pretty much a mystery. Like dinosaurs—perhaps the most famous and fearsome reptiles of all—they seem quite strange and very different from animals like mammals and birds.

There are several characteristics that set reptiles apart from other classes of animals. First, they have scaly skin. Second, they are what is known as ectothermic (cold-blooded). This means that they count on warmth from outside their own bodies— from the air, from water, and so on—to survive.

Of course, reptiles also have certain things in common with other animals. They have lungs for breathing and hearts that move their blood through their bodies. And they have a digestive system that processes the food they eat. To some degree they even have senses—sight, hearing, and so on—that give them information about the world.

Exactly why reptiles seem so strange, therefore, is something we can discover only by learning more about them.

Poisonous reptiles—like this beaded lizard—are definitely not recommended as pets.

Swift-moving geckos can be fun to watch as they dart from place to place.

Reptiles As Pets

The most popular reptile pets are lizards and snakes. Exactly which a person prefers depends on what he or she is like and finds interesting. For some, a swift-moving gecko is fascinating, and these people can spend hours watching it as it stalks around its tank. Others prefer snakes, especially snakes that are large enough to be handled and shown to friends.

To some degree, with reptiles smaller is sometimes better. Lizards and small snakes are, after all, easier to house and feed. Large snakes like boa constrictors and pythons can cause problems simply because of their size and appetites. Large lizards like iguanas are quite needy, and people may find it hard to lavish as much time and affection on a reptile as they would on a dog.

Choosing the right reptile is not just a matter of deciding how much you can afford to spend and how much space you have for a pet. It also is a matter of being honest with yourself about just how much you are willing to do with and for a pet.

Lizards

Some lizards are easy to care for and are well suited to even a beginning reptile owner. Some, however, may be too delicate or too aggressive for anyone but an experienced person. That is why it is so important to get lots of advice before buying any of these exotic pets and bringing them home.

One popular lizard is the leopard gecko, a small, ground-dwelling gecko. This is a friendly lizard that can be handled and that does not bite. It can be kept in a small fish tank—10 to 15 gallons (37.9 to 56.9 liters) furnished with sand, rocks, and some driftwood or small logs. The animal can be kept warm with a heat lamp or a heating pad placed under the tank.

Another small, easy-to-care-for lizard is the green anole. Three to five inches (7.6 to 12.7 centimeters) long, these creatures also can be kept in a glass tank. A few potted plants and some branches to climb on complete the environment. An ultraviolet light (which anoles need in order to survive) should be placed over the tank. As with a leopard gecko, a heating pad under the tank will help the anole stay warm.

The green anole is a popular pet that also is easy to care for.

Snakes

Many breeds of snakes make excellent pets. Corn snakes, for example, are one of the best pet snakes for a beginning reptile owner. Easy to care for, hardy, and friendly, they grow to between three and five feet (91.4 centimeters and 1.5 meters) long and can live quite comfortably in a glass tank. Shredded newspaper or wood shavings should cover the bottom. A "hide box" (a small enclosed area inside the tank) should be added to help the snake feel safe and comfortable.

Another good choice for a pet is the king snake. King snakes, which range in length from two to five feet (61 centimeters to 1.5 meters), require the same care as corn snakes. Milk snakes are closely related to king snakes and also make good pets.

Another popular pet is the ball python. These snakes will thrive in a 20-gallon (75.8-liter) tank with a heating pad and a hide box. People interested in owning ball pythons, however, should make sure their new pet was born in captivity. Ball pythons born in the wild can be aggressive. They also may not eat the food that is offered to them.

Corn snakes are one of the most common choices for people who want a pet snake.

Turtles come in all sizes, but most are best left in the wild.

Why Not Turtles?

Turtles would seem to be one of the easiest, least expensive pets of all. After all, they are frequently for sale, not just in pet stores but even in department and discount stores.

Surprisingly, however, turtles need a lot of care—more than many people have time to give. Aquatic turtles, in particular, are especially demanding. Because they live in water, they must have a complicated setup of filters, heaters, and ultraviolet lighting in order to stay healthy.

Still, turtles are cute and inexpensive to buy, so many people end up with them as pets without knowing what they are getting themselves into. In general, turtles should be left to experienced reptile owners.

Turtles come in all sizes and all prices. Common turtles sell for as little as thirty-five cents each; exotic turtles can cost more than a thousand dollars. Among the turtles commonly available are red-eared sliders and pond turtles, sometimes called aquatic barking turtles. Before buying a turtle, people should do some research and then buy only from a reputable dealer or pet store. This will help minimize the chances of getting either a diseased turtle or one that will grow too big to keep in a tank.

Choosing a Healthy Pet

It always is important to choose a healthy pet. This is especially true when dealing with reptiles. Of course, there is never any guarantee that a particular animal is in good health. But there are a few simple guidelines that can help.

First of all, the animal's eyes should be bright. The mouth should be clean and free from abscesses (collections of pus) and sores. The body should be "clean" too. In fact, some prospective owners actually run their hands along the reptile's body to check for bumps or bruises.

Another thing to avoid is a lizard whose nose is rubbed from pressing against the side of its aquarium. This is common and not always serious. But it may cause a disease called mouthrot.

There is no substitute for good advice from an expert before buying a pet reptile. Pet stores are a good source for information, as are experienced reptile owners. Libraries and the Internet are other sources for useful reference materials. Regardless of the source, the important thing is to ask questions— and to listen carefully for the answers.

Keeping track of its weight is a good way to check on an iguana's general health.

A Home within the Home

One of the most popular homes for a pet reptile is a glass tank with a screen top. These are easy to clean and give a clear view of the animal inside.

The size of the cage always should depend on the reptile. Geckos and arboreal snakes (snakes that live in trees) should be kept in tall tanks so they can climb freely and energetically. Ground dwelling reptiles probably will be happier and healthier in a low tank.

Tanks can be bought at a pet store, but many people choose to design and construct their own. Whatever type of tank is chosen, it is important to make sure to handle the animal carefully so that it does not escape. This is especially true in regard to geckos and other small lizards. These creatures are extremely fast on their feet, and once out of the tank they are almost impossible to capture.

For larger animals that can force open the lid, a cage clip is useful. (A cage clip is a lock designed specifically for aquariums with a screen top.) Bungee cords hooked around the tank and top are another reliable way to keep pet reptiles inside their home. Books or bricks on top of the screen top can work as long as the top can support the weight without caving in.

Tokay geckos are another popular choice among people who want small reptiles.

Habitats

To keep a pet reptile happy and healthy, owners generally try to re-create the animal's natural habitat inside its cage. For some owners this is part of the fun of owning an exotic reptile. For others an appropriate habitat is absolutely essential if the reptile is to survive in captivity.

It is not always necessary to match the animal's natural habitat precisely, of course. There is no need, for example, to use exactly the same plants that would be found in its habitat or even the same kind of soil. But some things—water, warmth, food, and a secure hiding place—are essential for just about all reptiles.

Desert lizards such as swifts, agamids, collared lizards, and chuckwallas can be kept in a cage with sand and rocks. They may not even need a water bowl.

Tropical snakes and lizards, boa constrictors, pythons, some colubrid (common, harmless) snakes, and anoles can be kept in a cage with foliage. Daily misting keeps the animals and plants comfortably moist.

*Owners often give a pet a habitat much like the one it
would have in the wild, complete with tree branches.*

Lighting

Reptiles need light in order to survive. Light provides warmth for these cold-blooded animals, and some reptiles also need ultraviolet rays to give them some of the vitamins they need.

Heat lamps can keep a pet warm, but care must be taken that a reptile's tank does not become too hot. If possible, the daily cycle of light should be similar to what the animal would experience in its natural habitat. Twelve hours of "daylight" are appropriate for reptiles from places near the equator where the days and nights are about the same amount of time. Species from temperate areas need a cycle with up to 16 hours of light a day in the summer and eight hours a day in the winter.

Timers can be used to run the lights, but owners must remember to change the times every few weeks to match the natural daylight cycle of the year. There are also electronic devices available that measure natural light from outside. These machines then duplicate the amount of light inside the reptile's cage.

Iguanas need more than just heat, light, and food.
They also need love and affection.

Heating

Reptiles are cold-blooded. That means that they need an outside source of heat to control their body temperature. Without a safe, reliable heat source, a pet reptile will die.

There are two recommended heat sources for reptiles. Fortunately, both of them are easy to obtain and use.

The first is called a basking light (to bask means to soak up the sun). Reptiles are natural sunbathers. But unlike people, who often end up getting painfully sunburned, reptiles know when to stop basking and seek shady shelter. This is why a cool hiding spot should be part of any pet reptile's home. It is also important to use a timer with a basking light so the proper amount of heat is given.

The second common heat source is a heating pad made specially for reptiles. These pads can be placed inside or underneath the cage. Some owners use both heating pads and heating lights together.

Cleaning

Reptile cages must be kept clean. This is not a matter of neatness. It is simply that in an unclean cage, the animal can get sick and die. A regular cleaning day—for example, every Monday evening—will help owners remember to do the cleaning at the proper time.

As a rule, the simpler the habitat, the simpler the cleaning job. In some cases cleanup may be as easy as changing the newspaper lining the bottom of the cage. In general, however, the water should be changed and the glass should be cleaned. Regular household cleaners contain chemicals that can make a reptile sick. So the glass should be wiped down with a glass cleaner made especially for reptile cages. (It can be purchased at most pet stores.) Sponges must be clean as well.

More complicated habitats need further care. Plants should be wiped with a clean, damp towel. Sand, bark chips, or lizard litter—which may be scattered on the bottom of the tank—needs to be cleaned or changed. Ornaments, branches, logs, and anything else in the tank should be cleaned as well.

The very first step in cleaning, however, always is to remove the pet reptile while its cage is being cleaned. The animal should be put into a comfortable, secure place from which it cannot escape.

*Some snakes—like this corn snake—need to
be fed live mice.*

Feeding

Some reptiles are herbivores, which means they eat only plants, fruits, and vegetables. Others eat only meat. (Meat eaters are called carnivores.) A number of reptiles, though, are omnivores, which means that they eat both meat and plants.

Responsible owners make sure they understand what foods their pets need in order to stay healthy and live long lives. As they feed their pets, reptile owners often notice that their animals have "favorite foods." If the animals don't make their favorites immediately clear, experimenting with different foods is the best way to learn what a particular reptile likes to eat.

People thinking about buying a carnivorous reptile, however, should be warned. Watching one of these reptiles eat is not for the squeamish. Some carnivorous reptiles eat insects and must be hand fed crickets or other living things. Other, larger reptiles eat rodents— from small mice to large rats. These too are fed to the animals live.

Reptile foods are available from pet stores. Depending on the size and appetite of the pet, this can get expensive. For this reason some reptile owners go so far as to collect wild insects or even breed their own mice or rats.

Handling Small Reptiles

Pet reptiles are easily bothered or annoyed, which can make them angry or even aggressive. For this reason they should be left alone as much as possible. But owners still need to know how to move or restrain their animals when cleaning their cage or moving them.

Most very small reptiles are quite delicate and can be easily injured. It is best to coax the small animal into a plastic container inside its cage and then remove the container. Care must be taken at all times that the animal does not escape.

Small lizards, such as anoles, should be held in the palm of the hand with the index finger behind the throat and the thumb on the animal's underside. The grip should be firm but light enough not to hurt the lizard.

Small to medium-sized snakes, such as corn and king snakes, should be grasped around the mid-body and on the neck directly behind the head. Then they can be lifted off the ground. Tame snakes can be allowed to glide through the hands.

Green anoles move so quickly that they can easily escape from an open tank or cage.

Handling Large Reptiles

Large lizards can easily hurt their human handlers, so extra care must be taken to avoid injury to either the lizard or its owner. Depending on the animal's size and temperament, more than one human handler may even be needed.

Iguanas, monitors, and other large lizards should be gripped firmly by the neck with one hand, with the other hand supporting its weight. The tail can be tucked under the arm so the lizard can't lash about. To prevent scratches, protective clothing and gloves should be worn.

Large snakes, such as boas and pythons, require especially careful handling, and they may require more than one handler. One person grasps the animal by the neck, and a second (and possibly third person) supports the snake's body. Snakes should never be allowed to drape themselves around someone's neck or wrap around a person's wrist.

When it is time to return the snake to its cage, the snake's body should be placed gently down on the floor of the cage, then released.

Reptiles should not be handled often. But when they are picked up, care must be taken not to harm them.

Shedding

All reptiles shed their skin. To do this, they need a rough surface to help them tear it off.

Snakes shed their skin in one piece, starting at the front and then moving down. As the snake moves free of its old skin, it leaves behind an inside-out or crumpled "copy" of the snake. Lizards, on the other hand, shed in pieces, tearing off bits of skin as the animals move around their cage. Sometimes they even pull off their own skin and eat it.

At times a lizard or snake has trouble shedding. An owner can help by putting the animal in lukewarm water to help soak the skin off. If this method is chosen, care must be taken that the animal does not drown. Placing moist sphagnum moss in the cage is another way to help the animal shed its skin. The moss—which can be bought at a garden supply store—helps soften the irritated skin.

Skin near a snake's eyes, called spectacles or eye shields, sometimes does not shed off easily. An owner can help remove a stuck spectacle by wrapping adhesive tape (sticky side out) around an index finger and dabbing lightly on the snake's eye.

Lizards often rub their skin against rough surfaces to help them shed.

Male or Female?

Determining the sex of a pet reptile is not always easy. In fact the males and females of a number of species look a lot alike.

Lizards are sometimes easy to tell apart because males usually have brighter colors than females. Males also have crests on their heads or dewlaps under their chins. These are flaps of skin that are used to attract females during mating time. Females are plainer in color. Also, certain pores on the underside of the back legs appear large on a male and small (or even absent) on a female.

With snakes it is harder to distinguish males from females. Males may have longer tails as well as bulges at the beginning of their tails. A male's tail may also have two rows—or sets—of scales instead of one. Female snakes may have a tail that tapers sharply from its base.

The sex of a snake can also be determined by a method called probing. This should be done only by a vet or other experienced professional.

Sometimes it takes a vet's knowing eye to find out whether a reptile is male or female.

Snakes and other reptiles can be difficult for the average pet owner to breed.

Breeding

Many reptile owners would like to breed their pets. Unfortunately, many common pet reptiles do not breed very easily in captivity. Still, it can be done if one follows a few general guidelines.

Learning the sex of the reptiles is only the first step. The health of the animals is important too. Only animals in good health can be bred successfully.

Owners also need to know exactly when their animals can breed. Some species can breed every month; others, just once a year. Some can breed only every few years.

It is also recommended that the sexes be kept separate except during the reptile's breeding season. This helps the animals realize that the other animal is not just a cagemate but a breeding mate of the opposite sex.

Care also should be taken to make sure the female and her offspring will be healthy. Some species require several seasons of steady feeding to gain enough fat to breed successfully. Others need additional vitamins and minerals to make sure that the eggs and babies are healthy and properly formed.

The Mating Game

Can you imagine a romantic iguana? Or a rattlesnake—even one without its fangs—asking another rattler out on a date? Strange but true, there actually may be a period of courtship before some reptiles mate.

Among some reptiles males may even compete with one another for the attentions of a female. For some this leads to a kind of courtship dance. For monitor lizards, on the other hand, there is a pushing and shoving contest. At the end of it the lizard that is pushed to the ground slinks away in defeat, while the winner mates with the female. When two male snakes are in the same cage with a female, they will lean against each other until one pushes the other down, pinning it to the ground.

Among reptiles the mating process itself can take anywhere from a few minutes to a few hours. Small male lizards, for example, often will nip at the female's neck, even to the point of leaving scars. In contrast, snakes may glide around the cage, the male's head behind the female's head. None of this may sound like old-fashioned traditional human romance. But to a snake or a lizard, it might be quite exciting.

It may seem hard to imagine, but some lizards actually puff themselves up or play romantic mating games to get attention from the opposite sex.

Incubating

A few reptiles give birth to live young, but most reptiles lay eggs. These eggs need to be incubated in order to hatch. Although human help is not needed in the wild, reptiles in captivity usually don't or can't incubate the eggs themselves.

In most cases the breeder will remove the eggs from the cage and incubate them in a container that holds moist sand or vermiculite, a common gardening supply. Most snakes and some lizards lay soft-shelled eggs. These should be partially buried in the material and kept moist. Hard-shelled eggs (most lizard eggs) don't need to be buried.

The eggs should be kept at approximately 72° to 80° Fahrenheit (22° to 27° Celsius). Any eggs that become moldy should be carefully removed without disturbing the other eggs.

In the cases of a few animals it may be better to leave the eggs in the cages. Gecko eggs, for example, are adhesive and may become stuck to the surface of the cage. If this happens, owners should not remove the eggs, which may break. Instead, owners should simply cover the eggs with a container for protection.

Geckos come in many different varieties and are becoming increasingly popular pets.

Rearing Young

Almost all babies—regardless of whether they are mammals, fish, or birds—need some special care during their early days. This is also true for reptiles. But exactly what young reptiles need from their parents varies from reptile to reptile. Their behavior varies as well.

Hatchling snakes, for example, often do not feed until after they have shed for the first time, which usually doesn't take place until four to ten days after hatching. Other young reptiles may hide until they are used to their surroundings. In general, keeping immature reptiles in small plastic containers can make it easier for the animals to find their food. It can also give owners a better view.

Young reptiles, like growing animals of all kinds, have different nutritional needs than adults. In addition to a steady diet they may need food supplements or vitamins. Young lizards need ultraviolet light too.

Reptile Shows

A reptile show or expo is a good place to start for someone interested in having a pet reptile. To begin with, these shows are an exciting way to learn more about reptiles. They also give people a chance to meet experienced reptile owners who can give useful advice on the care of their pets.

What goes on at these shows? At many of them owners bring reptiles to sell. There are also reptile books and reptile food for sale. In fact, a new owner could probably find at one of these shows everything needed to begin caring for a new reptile pet.

Reptile shows are also a good place to find exotic reptiles that are too unusual to see at local pet stores. Visitors can see these creatures and learn more about them, something they might otherwise be able to do only through magazines or books.

"Herp" Societies

Herpetology is the study of reptiles. Anyone who keeps reptiles as pets should seriously consider joining a herpetological society. These associations provide useful information and are also a way to meet people who share a common interest in reptiles and amphibians.

Most herp societies meet monthly and have an expo, or show, every year. Many mail out newsletters every month or two.

There are many herp societies in the United States, Canada, and all over the world. A listing of ones in various areas can be found in most reptile magazines, reptile shows, or zoos.

Owning a pet reptile is a big responsibility, but it can be rewarding and fun.

Responsibilities

Keeping a pet reptile is a big responsibility. If a reptile escapes in a neighborhood, people may become more upset than they would over a stray cat or dog. The danger to the animal's health is also an issue. It is unlikely that an escaped pet reptile will survive on its own. It may not be able to find the food or shelter it needs and die of starvation or cold. Or it may be attacked by wild animals or even other pets.

Some owners like to take their pet reptiles outside. But it is important to realize that many people either do not like reptiles or are afraid of them.

Pet reptiles also need daily care. Owners must be willing to spend as much time as needed to make sure their pets are healthy and active. They must also take care to arrange for a friend, relative, or neighbor to feed and water their pets when they are away on vacation.

Surprisingly, there are thousands of people who are willing to do all this and more. To them reptiles are an exciting—and in a way a lovable—kind of pet.

Words to Know

Abscesses   Sores or holes in the body.

Aquatic   Living in the water.

Basking light   A lamp or bulb that provides reptiles with light and warmth.

Bungee cords   Stretchable cords that can be used to fasten things securely.

Cage clip   A lock that holds the screen lid of a reptile cage securely closed.

Carnivore   A creature that eats meat.

Ectothermic   Cold-blooded, meaning that the animal's body temperature changes according to the temperature of its surroundings.

Hatchlings   Creatures that have just recently hatched from their eggs.

Herbivore   A creature that eats only plants, fruits, and vegetables.

Herpetology   The study of reptiles.

Incubator   A machine that keeps an egg or young living thing warm until it is ready to hatch or be on its own.

Lizard litter   Material available in pet stores and used to line the bottom of reptile tanks or cages.

Omnivore   A creature that eats both meat and plants.

Probing   Use of a metal rod to find out the sex of a snake; a process that should be carried out only by a vet or other trained professional.

Spectacles   Also called eye shields; skin near the eyes of a reptile.

Ultraviolet   Light that is beyond the color violet in the spectrum.

Wood shavings   Chips of wood that can be used to line the bottom of a pet cage.

INDEX

Cover Photo: Wildlife Conservation Society
Photo Credits: Norvia Behling (Behling & Johnson Photography), pages 17, 35; Rick &
Nora Bowers (The Wildlife Collection), page 8; John Guistina (The Wildlife Collection),
pages 19, 21, 33; Martin Harvey (The Wildlife Collection), pages 39, 41; Clay Myers (The
Wildlife Collection), page 29; Lynn M. Stone, pages 7, 13, 14, 31; SuperStock, Inc., pages 4,
36, 45; Wildlife Conservation Society, pages 11, 22, 26.